READING POWER

Technology That Changed the World

The Steam Engine
Fueling the Industrial Revolution

Joanne Mattern

The Rosen Publishing Group's
PowerKids Press™
New York

Published in 2003 by The Rosen Publishing Group, Inc.
29 East 21st Street, New York, NY 10010

First Edition

Book Design: Michael DeLisio

Photo Credits: Cover © Minnesota Historical Society/Corbis; pp. 5, 7, 14, 15, 16, 18, 19 © Culver Pictures; pp. 8, 9 © North Wind Picture Archives; pp.10–11 © Corbis; pp. 13 Michael DeLisio; p. 17 © Bettmann/ Corbis; p. 21 © Charles E. Rotkin/Corbis

Library of Congress Cataloging-in-Publication Data

Mattern, Joanne, 1963-
The steam engine : fueling the Industrial Revolution / Joanne Mattern.
    p. cm. — (Technology that changed the world)
Summary: Presents information on the steam engine, including its invention, history, how it works, and how it has affected people's lives.
Includes bibliographical references and index.
ISBN 0-8239-6490-6 (library binding)
1. Steam-engines—History. [1. Steam engines.] I. Title.
TJ461 .M435 2003
621.1—dc21
                                          2002000502

Contents

The Need for Power 4

The First Steam Engines 6

Improving the Steam Engine 8

The Power of Steam 12

Steam Engines at Work 14

Glossary 22

Resources 23

Index/Word Count 24

Note 24

The Need for Power

Many years ago, coal was one of the most important kinds of fuels. People dug mines deep into the earth to reach the coal. The mines would often get filled with water. The need to keep mines dry led to the making of the steam engine—one of the most important inventions ever made.

Now You Know

A scientist in Alexandria, Egypt, wrote about the first steam engine around 60 A.D. However, this steam engine did no useful work.

Coal miners at work

The First Steam Engines

In 1698, Thomas Savery made a steam engine to run a pump to get water out of the mines where miners worked. He called this steam-powered pump the Miner's Friend. In 1712, Thomas Newcomen made a better steam engine to run the pump. By the 1730s, Newcomen's engines were used in several countries.

Savery's steam engine

Improving the Steam Engine

In 1763, James Watt thought of a way to make a better steam engine. He got his idea while fixing a Newcomen steam engine.

James Watt was born in Scotland in 1736. His work on the steam engine made him very rich.

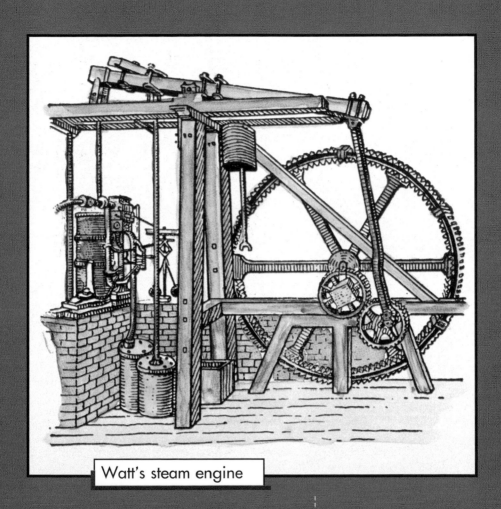

Watt's steam engine

Now You Know

Electrical power is measured in watts. Watts are named after James Watt.

At first, Watt's steam engine was used only to power the pumps that were used in the mines. By 1790, his steam engine was being used to run many machines in factories all over England. The steam engine was helping the Industrial Revolution grow.

Cotton mills used Watt's steam engine to power the machines that made cloth. These factories no longer had to be near fast-moving rivers to use water power to run their machinery. Steam engines made it possible for factories to be built anywhere.

The Power of Steam

Steam engines work by using the power of steam. A boiler heats water until it becomes steam. As more steam is made, it can spin a turbine or push a piston back and forth. This movement is used to make energy, such as electricity, or to move the parts of other machines.

There are many different types of steam engines. This picture shows one way a steam engine with a piston works.

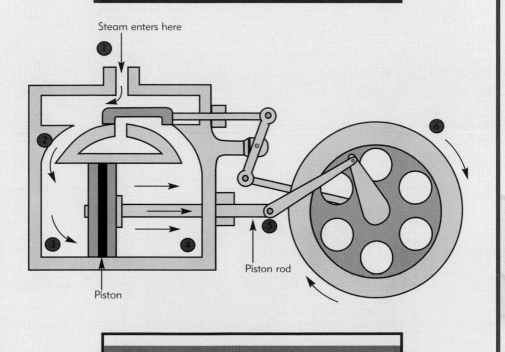

Steam enters here

Piston

Piston rod

How a Steam Engine Works

1. Steam is put into the engine.

2. Steam moves through the engine.

3. Steam pushes against a piston.

4. The piston moves forward.

5. The piston moves a piston rod.

6. The piston rod turns the moving part of the machine that the steam engine is powering, such as the wheels of a locomotive train.

Steam Engines at Work

In the early 1800s, Richard Trevithick made a steam engine strong enough to power the first steam locomotive. In 1807, Robert Fulton made the first successful steamer, or steam-powered boat. In 1819, the *Savannah* was the first steamship to cross the Atlantic Ocean.

Robert Fulton

On August 18, 1807, Robert Fulton's steamer, *the* Clermont, *traveled 150 miles from New York City to Albany, New York.*

The Savannah *sailed from New York City to Liverpool, England.*

In 1829, George and Robert Stephenson made the *Rocket* steam locomotive. The *Rocket* went as fast as 29 miles an hour. The *Rocket* was the first vehicle to travel faster than a horse.

The success of the Rocket proved that steam-powered locomotives could be used for railroads.

Before he built the Rocket, George Stephenson made locomotives to move coal in mines.

In 1897, twin brothers Francis and Freelan Stanley made the first car that used a steam engine. They called their car the Stanley Steamer.

Now You Know

The Stanleys used their cars in auto races. One of their cars went as fast as 128 miles an hour.

The Stanley Brothers' racecar

*The Stanley brothers go for a ride
in one of their steam-powered cars.*

Machines that were powered by steam engines did the hard work that people could not do. Steam-powered cars, trains, and boats moved people and goods fast over long distances. Steam engines ran machines in factories. Steam-powered machines helped people build cities.

The steam engine changed the way people lived and worked.

Time Line	
A.D. 60:	A scientist in Egypt writes about the first steam engine.
1698:	Thomas Savery makes a steam engine to power a pump to get water out of mines.
1712:	Thomas Newcomen makes a better steam engine.
1763:	James Watt begins improving the Newcomen engine.
1785:	The steam engine is first used in a cotton mill.
1804:	Richard Trevithick makes the first steam engine to power a train.
1807:	Robert Fulton's steamboat, the *Clermont*, makes its first trip from New York City to Albany.
1819:	The *Savannah* is the first steamship to cross the Atlantic Ocean.
1829:	The *Rocket* steam locomotive is invented by George and Robert Stephenson.
1897:	The first steam-powered car, the Stanley Steamer, is built.

Today, some power plants use steam engines to power turbines.

Glossary

boiler (**boi**-luhr) a part of a steam engine that heats water

electricity (ih-lehk-**trihs**-uh-tee) a form of power used to make light, heat, or motion

energy (**ehn**-uhr-jee) power that can be used to produce heat or make machines work

fuels (**fyoo**-uhlz) things that are burned to produce heat or power

Industrial Revolution (ihn-**duhs**-tree-uhl rehv-uh-**loo**-shuhn) a slow change from handmade tools and home manufacturing to power-driven tools and large-scale factory production

inventions (ihn-**vehn**-shuhnz) new things that are made or thought of

locomotive (loh-kuh-**moh**-tihv) a large engine that moves under its own power and is used to pull railroad trains

mill (**mihl**) a building with machinery for making things

piston (**pihs**-tuhn) a sliding piece that moves back and forth against water pressure

steam engine (**steem ehn**-juhn) a machine that works by steam power

turbine (**ter**-buhn) a machine driven by water or steam passing through blades on a wheel

vehicle (**vee**-hih-kuhl) something used to carry people or things

Resources

Books

James Watt
by Neil Champion
Heinemann Library (2000)

The Industrial Revolution
by Mary Collins
Children's Press (2000)

Web Sites

Due to the changing nature of Internet links, PowerKids
Press has developed an online list of Web sites related
to the subjects of this book. This site is updated regularly.
Please use this link to access the list:

http://www.powerkidslinks.com/tcw/steam/

Index

B
boiler, 12

E
electricity, 12
energy, 12

F
factories, 10–11, 20

I
Industrial Revolution, 10
inventions, 4

L
locomotive, 13–14,
     16–17, 20

M
mill, 11, 20

P
piston, 12–13

R
Rocket, 16–17, 20

S
Stanley, Francis and
     Freelan, 18–19
steam engine, 4, 6–14,
     18, 20–21
Stephenson, George
     and Robert, 16, 20

T
turbine, 12, 21

V
vehicle, 16

Word Count: 474

Note to Librarians, Teachers, and Parents

If reading is a challenge, Reading Power is a solution! Reading Power is perfect for readers who want high-interest subject matter at an accessible reading level. These fact-filled, photo-illustrated books are designed for readers who want straightforward vocabulary, engaging topics, and a manageable reading experience. With clear picture/text correspondence, leveled Reading Power books put the reader in charge. Now readers have the power to get the information they want and the skills they need in a user-friendly format.